SECOND EDITION

TOUCHSTONE

WORKBOOK 3B

MICHAEL MCCARTHY
JEANNE MCCARTEN
HELEN SANDIFORD

CAMBRIDGE
UNIVERSITY PRESS

University Printing House, Cambridge CB2 8BS, United Kingdom

One Liberty Plaza, 20th Floor, New York, NY 10006, USA

477 Williamstown Road, Port Melbourne, VIC 3207, Australia

314–321, 3rd Floor, Plot 3, Splendor Forum, Jasola District Centre, New Delhi – 110025, India

79 Anson Road, #06–04/06, Singapore 079906

Cambridge University Press is part of the University of Cambridge.

It furthers the University's mission by disseminating knowledge in the pursuit of education, learning, and research at the highest international levels of excellence.

www.cambridge.org
Information on this title: www.cambridge.org/9781107651470

© Cambridge University Press 2005, 2014

This publication is in copyright. Subject to statutory exception and to the provisions of relevant collective licensing agreements, no reproduction of any part may take place without the written permission of Cambridge University Press.

First published 2005
Second Edition 2014
20 19 18 17 16 15 14 13 12 11 10 9 8 7 6 5

Printed in the United Kingdom by Latimer Trend

A catalog record for this publication is available from the British Library.

ISBN 978-1-107-66583-5 Student's Book
ISBN 978-1-107-62875-5 Student's Book A
ISBN 978-1-107-69446-0 Student's Book B
ISBN 978-1-107-64271-3 Workbook
ISBN 978-1-107-62082-7 Workbook A
ISBN 978-1-107-65147-0 Workbook B
ISBN 978-1-107-62794-9 Full Contact
ISBN 978-1-107-63739-9 Full Contact A
ISBN 978-1-107-63903-4 Full Contact B
ISBN 978-1-107-68094-4 Teacher's Edition with Assessment Audio CD/CD-ROM
ISBN 978-1-107-63179-3 Class Audio CDs (4)

Additional resources for this publication at www.cambridge.org/touchstone2

Cambridge University Press has no responsibility for the persistence or accuracy of URLs for external or third-party internet websites referred to in this publication, and does not guarantee that any content on such websites is, or will remain, accurate or appropriate. Information regarding prices, travel timetables, and other factual information given in this work is correct at the time of first printing but Cambridge University Press does not guarantee the accuracy of such information thereafter.

Contents

7 Relationships 50

8 What if? 58

9 Tech savvy? 66

10 What's up? 74

11 Impressions 82

12 In the news 90

Relationships

UNIT 7

Lesson A Circle of friends

1 He's the guy . . .

Grammar **Choose the correct relative pronoun to complete each sentence. If a relative pronoun is not needed, circle the dash (—).**

1. This is Andrew. He's the guy **which** / (—) I met on vacation in Florida.

2. This is the dog **that** / **who** followed me on the beach one day. It turned out to be Andrew's dog. So I guess it was the dog **that** / — introduced us.

3. This is the amusement park **who** / — we went to on our first date. And this is the ticket for the first movie **that** / **who** we saw.

4. Here's the necklace **that** / **who** he gave me before I left for home. Andrew is someone **which** / **who** I'm going to keep in touch with.

5. This is the letter **that** / — came three days after I got back. Inside is the photo **who** / — he took of me the day I left.

6. We talk every day. And this is the phone bill **who** / **that** I got yesterday!

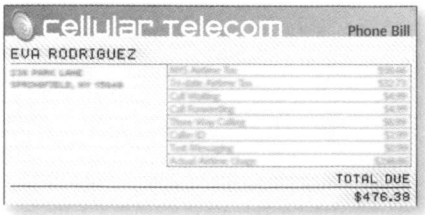

2 She's the girl . . .

Grammar **Complete the email with *who*, *that*, or *which*. Put the word in parentheses ( ) if the sentence is also complete without the relative pronoun. Sometimes more than one answer is possible.**

New Message

To: mel_bes@cup.com
From: camilleS@cup.com
Subject: Estella and Ramiro

Dear Melania,

I'm so excited about some news *(that / which)* I just got from a friend. You know Estella, right? She's my friend from Peru _____ I met in college. Well, last year I introduced her to that cute guy, Ramiro, _____ I used to work with. He had the desk _____ was across from mine. Anyway, a group of us used to go out together sometimes after work. One day, I invited Estella along. (I knew Ramiro was exactly the kind of guy _____ she would like.) We went to the Caribbean restaurant _____ I love on Essex Street. To make a long story short, they met that night, and now they're getting married. I just got the invitation. I can't wait for the wedding!

Camille

3 I have a friend . . .

Grammar **Use the sentences in the box and *who*, *that*, or *which* to complete the sentences below. Put the relative pronoun in parentheses ( ) if the sentence is also complete without it. Sometimes more than one answer is possible.**

Her family owns a store.	It served traditional Korean food.	The paper has rose petals in it.
I spoke to her in Korean.	✓She lives in South Korea.	The shop sells handmade paper.

1. I have a friend, Seung-Li, *who / that lives in South Korea* _____.
2. I met her in Seoul at the store _____.
3. It is a very special shop _____.
4. I bought some paper _____.
5. She was the only person _____.
6. Later, she invited me to a restaurant _____.

4 About you

Grammar **Complete the sentences with true information. Use relative pronouns where necessary.**

1. I have a friend *who speaks three languages* _____.
2. My neighbor is someone _____.
3. I like stores _____.
4. I take a class _____.
5. I don't like the food _____.
6. I know someone _____.

1 Which particle?

Grammar and vocabulary

Circle the correct particle to complete each sentence.

1. My sister's not home. She went **up** / **away** / **along** for the weekend.
2. I grew **out** / **down** / **up** in Morocco, but now I live in California.
3. My brother isn't ready to settle **out** / **up** / **down**. He doesn't want to get married yet.
4. My mother's away on business now, but she plans to fly **away** / **along** / **back** next Tuesday.
5. I thought I had a doctor's appointment today, but it turns **out** / **up** / **down** that it's next week.
6. My best friend is moving **up** / **away** / **along** next month. I'm going to miss her.
7. I forgot to sign **back** / **out** / **up** for the class trip to the museum, so I can't go.
8. I sent my cousin an email last week, but he never wrote **back** / **away** / **out**.

2 Figure it out!

Grammar and vocabulary

Complete the sentences with the phrasal verbs in the box. Then complete the puzzle and the sentence below.

come back	go away	sign up	✓write back
get along	grow up	work out	

1. When a friend sends you an email, you should *write back* immediately.
2. If a relationship doesn't _____, don't worry about it. It may be for the best.
3. If you want to _____ well with someone, be a good friend!
4. It's good to take a break from your usual routine and _____ for a few days.
5. It's fun to go on vacation, but it's always good to _____ home, too!
6. A lot of kids _____ in blended families these days.
7. One way to meet new people is to _____ for a class.

1. w r i t e [b] a c k
2. ___ ___ [ ] ___ ___ ___ ___
3. ___ [ ] ___ ___ ___ ___ ___ ___
4. ___ ___ [ ] ___ ___ ___
5. ___ ___ ___ ___ ___ ___ ___ [ ]
6. ___ ___ ___ ___ [ ] ___
7. ___ ___ ___ ___ ___ [ ]

Some couples like to _____ _____ because they think it's fun to make up and get back together!

3 Breaking up is hard to do.

Grammar and vocabulary

Complete the conversation with the correct form of the phrasal verbs in the box. Sometimes more than one answer is possible.

✓break up	go out	turn out
get along	hang out	work out

Tina Hi, Jorge. You don't look so good. What's wrong?

Jorge Well, my girlfriend and I *broke up* last week.

Tina Oh, no. You did? That's too bad. How long were you _____ with her?

Jorge About three months. I can't believe things didn't _____. I mean, we _____ really well. I thought everything was fine.

Tina Yeah, you guys were always _____ together.

Jorge I know. We saw each other almost every day!

Tina Well, maybe that was the problem. Maybe she didn't want to spend every minute of every day with you.

Jorge Yeah, I guess you're right. Things didn't _____ the way I thought.

Tina Why don't you talk to her? Ask her what she wants in a relationship.

4 About you

Grammar and vocabulary

Answer the questions with true information.

1. Who do you get along well with? Why?
   I get along well with my sister because we are very similar.

2. Do you like to go away for summer vacation?
   _____

3. Where do you and your friends like to hang out?
   _____

4. Do you always write back immediately when someone sends you an email?
   _____

5. Are there any classes you would like to sign up for?
   _____

6. Do you think you'll ever move far away from home?
   _____

Lesson C She's just a bit odd.

1 I guess . . .

Conversation strategies

Rewrite each sentence with the two "softening" expressions in parentheses to complete the conversations.

1. A What's wrong with Jamil? He just yelled at me for turning on the TV.

   B *He's probably just tired.* He stayed
   He's tired. (probably / just)

   up all night. He had to finish a paper for school.

   A He always waits until the last minute to do his work.

   B I know. _____
   He's disorganized. (I guess / kind of)

   A Yeah, and he has so many activities at school.

   _____
   He's doing too much. (I think / a bit)

   B But it's good to be involved with your school.

   A That's true. _____
   He's stressed out. (I guess / sort of)

2. A Have you met Alissa yet? She's the new student in our class.

   B Yeah. I talked to her yesterday, but she didn't say much.

   A _____
   She's shy. (maybe / just)

   B Yeah, I'm sure she'll meet people soon.

   _____
   It takes time. (just / a little)

   A It's difficult when you don't know anyone.

   B I know. _____
   It's hard to fit in. (I think / sort of)

   A Yeah. _____
   Making friends is hard. (I guess / in a way)

2 It's spicy, though.

Conversation strategies

Complete the conversations with the responses in the box. Add *though* if appropriate.

He's pretty shy.	I'll find out when he's free.
He's here for two weeks.	It was a little spicy.
✓ I love Thai food.	It was really nice.

1. Lee How was your dinner date last night?
   Kyra Great. We went to a Thai restaurant that Wayne knows.
   Lee Cool. *I love Thai food.* What did you have?
   Kyra Green curry with chicken and a vegetable dish.
   Lee Was it good?
   Kyra Yeah, the food was excellent. _____
   I don't usually like spicy food, but I really enjoyed it.
   Lee Was it expensive?
   Kyra Well, it was a little expensive. _____

2. Becky Brad, who's the new guy in your department?
   Brad Oh, that's Bart. He's just visiting from the Los Angeles office. _____
   Becky Only two weeks? That's too bad. He seems interesting.
   Brad Yeah. _____ He's probably kind of lonely.
   Becky Well, maybe we should invite him to dinner. Then we could show him around a little before he leaves.
   Brad That sounds like a great idea. _____

3 About you

Conversation strategies

Use true information to answer each set of questions. Respond to the first question using "softening" comments. Then respond to the second question using *though*.

1. What's something you're bad at? What's something you're good at?
   I guess I'm kind of bad at playing tennis. I'm really great at playing chess, though.
2. What's your worst quality? What's your best quality?
   _____
3. What's difficult about learning English? What do you like about learning English?
   _____
4. What annoying habit does one of your friends have? What's nice about him or her?
   _____
5. What's your least favorite kind of music? What's your favorite kind?
   _____

1 Interactive communities

Reading **A Read the article. What topics are discussed? Check (✓) all that apply.**

☐ dating sites ☐ meeting people offline ☐ phone apps ☐ social networking

Using the online world to go offline

With our ability to connect to almost anyone in the world at any time, are we feeling more alone than ever? That's the question that critics of technology are asking. Some research suggests that people who use the Internet and social networks a lot often feel isolated and lonelier than people who don't. Supporters of online socializing disagree and point out that it's up to the user whether or not an online relationship becomes a meaningful, face-to-face one. After all, social networks, Internet companies, and app developers are merely doing their job – connecting users online. The next steps from online to offline are for us, the users, to take.

In fact, social networking websites often give us all the tools we need to move easily from an online relationship to an offline one. For example, there are websites that organize groups around particular interests. Perhaps you've just moved to a new city and want to meet people who have the same interests as you. You can sign up on websites that help you find others who enjoy the same hobbies. Many of these groups plan face-to-face activities. It's a great way to connect with people you would never meet otherwise. There's no guarantee that you'll get along, but at least you'll have something in common.

Apps for cell phones or tablets can also help us connect with people offline in several ways. Some apps let you find friends nearby, find out what they are doing, and who's available to hang out. Other apps help you plan activities. You can send an invitation to friends electronically and include details about the activity, maps, and directions for how to get there. The people you invite can respond in the same way. There are also apps that recommend where you can meet people, for example, at restaurants or museums.

Technology doesn't have to isolate us. There are plenty of websites and phone apps that help us create social networks, both online and in real life. The trick is to make the effort. At some point, we have to pull our attention away from the screen in order to actually meet someone.

B Read the article again. Are the sentences true, false, or is the information not given? Write *T* (true), *F* (false), or *D* (doesn't say).

1. People who spend too much time online can feel lonely. __T__
2. The writer suggests that social networks are to blame for people's loneliness. ____
3. Websites that are for people with similar interests connect people that get along. ____
4. If you sign up for a website that organizes face-to-face activities, you'll meet new people that you like. ____
5. Most people only want to use websites and apps to find dates, not to find friends. ____
6. Technology can improve your relationships with your circle of friends. ____

2 Common ground

Writing **A** **Read the email. Then complete the sentences with *both*, *both of us*, or *neither of us*.**

New Message

To: mitch_88@cup.com
From: PhilJ@cup.com
Subject: Your high school friend

Dear Mitch,

Remember me from high school? I'm the guy who sat behind you in world literature class. I got your email address from Kurt, the guy we ___both___ used to hang out with at lunchtime.

I'll always remember that class. _____ hated reading those short stories, but we had to take the class for some reason. And _____ liked our teacher, Mr. What's-his-name. He wasn't a very good teacher at all. It's amazing that we _____ passed the final exam. Good thing we _____ stayed up late studying the night before.

Anyway, I was talking to Kurt last week, and _____ would like to see you again. Maybe we can all meet and go out for dinner or something one day soon.

Take care,
Phil

B **Write an email to an old friend you haven't seen in a long time. Include things you did and didn't have in common.**

New Message

To: buddy1@cup.com
From: buddy2@cup.com
Subject: Long time no see!

_____

_____

_____

_____

Unit 7 Progress chart

	What can you do? Mark the boxes. ✓ = I can . . . ? = I need to review how to . . .	To review, go back to these pages in the Student's Book.
Grammar	☐ write sentences with subject and object relative clauses. ☐ use phrasal verbs like *grow up*, *get along*, and *break up*.	66 and 67 68 and 69
Vocabulary	☐ use at least 12 phrasal verbs.	68 and 69
Conversation strategies	☐ use at least 6 expressions to soften comments. ☐ give a contrasting idea using *though*.	70 71
Writing	☐ use *both*, *both of us*, and *neither of us*.	73

What if?

UNIT 8

Lesson A Wishes

1 When you wish . . .

Grammar **A** What are these people wishing for right now? Complete the sentences.

1. James *wishes he had a new car* .

2. Emi and Sue _____ .

3. Joey _____ .

4. Esteban and Pilar _____ .

5. Al _____ .

6. Li-ming _____ .

B Complete the sentences about the people in part A.

1. If James *had* (have) more money, he *would buy* (buy) a new car.
2. If Emi and Sue _____ (live) in a bigger apartment, they _____ (have) more space.
3. If Joey _____ (be) taller, he _____ (score) more points.
4. If Esteban and Pilar _____ (have) two TVs, they _____ (not have) to watch the same TV shows.
5. If Al _____ (not be) a bad cook, he _____ (eat) better.
6. If Li-ming _____ (live) in the country, she _____ (be) much happier.

2 About you

Grammar **Write true sentences about your wishes.**

My Wish List

1. I wish I *had more free time during the week*. (have)
   If I *had more free time during the week, I'd exercise more*. (have)
2. I wish I _____. (be)
   If I _____. (be)
3. I wish I _____. (can)
   If I _____. (can)
4. I wish I _____. (not be)
   If I _____. (not be)
5. I wish my parents _____. (not be)
   If they _____. (not be)
6. I wish my friend _____. (be)
   If he or she _____. (be)
7. I wish I _____. (have)
   If I _____. (have)
8. I wish I _____. (not have to)
   If I _____. (not have to)
9. I wish I _____. (live)
   If I _____. (live)

1 If I had a problem, . . .

Vocabulary **Circle the correct word to complete each sentence. Then decide if each sentence is true or false for you. Write *T* (true) or *F* (false). Correct the false statements.**

1. F If I had a problem, I would talk **for** / (**to**) / **about** my best friend.
   If I had a problem, I would talk to my Aunt Lisa.
2. ____ I always apologize **about** / **to** / **for** my mistakes.
   _____
3. ____ My friends never thank me **for** / **about** / **with** helping them.
   _____
4. ____ I always worry **for** / **about** / **from** taking tests!
   _____
5. ____ I often share books **to** / **with** / **about** my neighbors.
   _____
6. ____ If I forgot **with** / **from** / **about** a friend's birthday, I would feel bad.
   _____

2 Remind me about it.

Vocabulary **Complete the conversations with the words in the box.**

ask for	✓forget about	remind about	worry about
borrow from	lend to	talk to	
buy for	pay for	think about	

1. A Where's Marissa? I hope she didn't *forget* *about* our party.
   B I know. Let's call her and _____ her _____ it.
2. A Oh, no. I forgot my wallet. Can I _____ some money _____ you for lunch?
   B Oh, don't _____ _____ it. I'll get lunch. It's my treat!
3. A Do you think I should _____ this camera _____ my sister's birthday?
   B Why don't you _____ _____ her about it first?
4. A Can you _____ ten dollars _____ Lenny to buy a movie ticket?
   B I'm sorry. I can't. I have just enough to _____ _____ my own ticket.
5. A I think we're lost. Should we _____ someone _____ directions to the museum?
   B Not yet. I'm sure if I _____ _____ it for a minute, I'll remember how to get there.

3 Would you ask for an autograph?

Grammar **Complete the questions with the correct form of the verbs.**

1. What *would you say* (say) if you *met* (meet) a famous athlete?
   Would you ask (ask) for an autograph?
2. If you _____ (see) an accident, what _____ (do)?
   _____ (call) for an ambulance?
3. What _____ (do) if you _____ (have) a large spider on your leg? _____ (scream)?
4. If you _____ (break) your best friend's camera, how _____ (feel)? _____ (offer) to replace it?
5. How _____ (react) if your best friend _____ (win) a trip to Hawai'i? _____ (feel) jealous?
6. What _____ (say) to your neighbors if they _____ (complain) about your music? _____ (apologize)?

4 About you

Grammar **Answer the questions in Exercise 3. Write true information.**

1. *If I met a famous athlete, I'd say, "I really admire you!" I would definitely ask for an autograph.*
2. _____
3. _____
4. _____
5. _____
6. _____

Lesson C If I were you, . . .

1 I'd choose . . .

Conversation strategies **Complete the conversation with the expressions in the box. Sometimes more than one answer is possible.**

✓if I were you, I'd	I would	I wouldn't	you could	you might want to

Serge I really want to take a vacation this summer, but I need to work, too.

Nina Well, *if I were you, I'd* take a vacation first. You might not get another chance.

Serge Hmm. Maybe I should. Where's a good place to go – any ideas?

Nina Well, there are so many great places. I mean, _____ go anywhere. Have you been to Europe?

Serge No. I'd love to. It's kind of expensive, though.

Nina Well, _____ let that stop you! Seriously, you can always get a job there. There are programs for students who want to work abroad. _____ find out about them if I were you.

Serge I never thought of that.

Nina _____ look on the Internet and do a little research.

Serge Yeah. That's a great idea. So, I could work *and* take a vacation.

2 Good advice

Conversation strategies **Grace is having a bad day. Respond to her statements with advice.**

1. **Grace** I didn't do very well on my math exam.
   You *If I were you, I'd talk to the teacher.*
2. **Grace** Ouch! I just got a bad paper cut.
   You _____
3. **Grace** Oh, no! My car won't start.
   You _____
4. **Grace** I just stained my favorite sweater.
   You _____

3 You might want to . . .

Conversation strategies **Look at the pictures. Complete the advice.**

1. You look tired. *I would get some coffee* _____.

2. The sun's really strong. I _____ _____.

3. It's very windy. If _____ _____.

4. It's very cold. You _____ _____.

4 That would be fun.

Conversation strategies **Respond to each sentence with *That would be* and an appropriate adjective.**

1. I'd really like to hike in the Himalayas. — *Wow. That would be awesome!*
2. Maybe we could go to the mall this afternoon. — _____
3. It would be great to win a million dollars. — _____
4. One day, I'm going to learn to tango. — _____

1 What do you regret?

Reading **A** **Read the article about regrets. According to the article, which of the following factors affect how people regret things in life?**

☐ age ☐ climate ☐ culture ☐ gender ☐ health ☐ income

Regrets? Too few to mention

Do you ever lie awake at night with regrets? Do you spend hours wishing you could change your life? __5__ If so, you're not alone. Regret – that negative feeling you have after a bad experience – is a fairly common human emotion. However, recent research suggests that while almost everyone experiences regret at some point or another, it is much more negative for some than for others.

What do we regret? According to research, we tend to regret decisions we made about our education, careers, romance, and parenting. We feel bad about things we did. ____ We wish we had different life opportunities, could make different choices, and relive moments with different outcomes. However, the nature and impact of regrets can vary across ages, sex, and cultures.

From the research, it would seem that the most striking difference in how regret affects people is between younger and older people. Younger people tend to regret the things they actually did, whereas older people regret the things they didn't do – their missed opportunities. Older people experience regret much more negatively. ____ Younger people are more likely to see a bad experience as an important learning opportunity. They realize they made a mistake, and they use that to guide their decisions in the future. Older people don't feel they have the same chance to correct their actions and their outcomes.

Gender and culture can also affect what and how we regret. ____ According to some research, more women may regret lost romantic opportunities and family conflicts. More men may regret their decisions around career, money, and education. In cultures that put a high value on personal choice, such as the United States, people tend to have more regrets. In cultures where the family or the community makes more decisions, people have fewer regrets. Research suggests that the more choices we have, the more possibilities we have to regret.

So, if you find yourself staring at the ceiling at 3 a.m., what can you do to turn your regret into something positive? Use it to make better choices in the future. Realize that you couldn't control everything in the past situation. Take more chances in the future. ____ And be a little easier on yourself.

B **Read the article again. Then add these missing sentences to the article by writing each number in the correct blank.**

1. The differences between men and women are interesting.
2. We may feel worse about the things we didn't do.
3. Have more fun.
4. It can even lead to depression in some older people.
5. Do you torture yourself thinking about your mistakes?

C **Choose the correct options to complete the sentences.**

1. Feeling regret is **not common** / **normal**.
2. The feeling of regret is **worse for some** / **the same for everyone**.
3. Older people mostly regret things they **did** / **didn't do**.
4. **Younger** / **Older** people feel they are in a better position to avoid the same mistakes.
5. Regret is **more** / **less** common when people make their own decisions.
6. The article suggests that in the end, regret is **useless** / **useful**.

2 If I won the lottery, . . .

Writing **A** **Read the journal entry. Complete the sentences with the adverbs given and the correct verb forms.**

If I won the lottery, I 'd definitely quit (definitely / quit) my job, and I _____ (probably / not work) at all! If I were a millionaire, I _____ (definitely / buy) a house on the beach and one in the mountains. If I had two houses, I _____ (definitely / invite) my family and friends to visit, but I _____ (probably / not invite) them every weekend. I'd want some time for myself. If I had more time for myself, I'd write more, and I _____ (probably / try) to publish a book. What would the title of the book be? "How to Live Like a Millionaire," of course!

B **Write a journal entry about what you would do if you were a millionaire. Use *definitely* and *probably* to show degrees of certainty.**

_____

_____

_____

Unit 8 Progress chart

What can you do? Mark the boxes. ✓ = I can . . . ? = I need to review how to . . .	To review, go back to these pages in the Student's Book.
Grammar	
☐ use *wish* + past form of verb for wishes about the present or future.	76 and 77
☐ use *If* + past form of verb, followed by *would* / *could* + verb to talk about imaginary situations in the present or future.	76, 77, and 79
Vocabulary	
☐ use the correct preposition after at least 12 verbs.	78
Conversation strategies	
☐ give advice using expressions like *If I were you* and *You could*.	80
☐ use *That would be* to comment on a possibility or a suggestion.	81
Writing	
☐ use *definitely* and *probably* to show degrees of certainty.	83

Tech savvy?

UNIT 9

Lesson A Tech support

1 I have no idea why . . .

Grammar **A Unscramble the questions.**

1. which battery / Do you know / should / buy / I / ?
   Do you know which battery I should buy?
2. they / where / are / Can you tell me / ?
   _____
3. when / you / Can you remember / it / last changed / ?
   _____
4. it / Do you have any idea / how much / costs / ?
   _____

B Unscramble the statements.

1. why / isn't / I have no idea / working / it
   _____
2. last changed it / when / I don't know / I
   _____
3. two / I / if / I wonder / should / batteries / buy
   _____

C Complete the conversation with the questions and statements from parts A and B.

Woman Excuse me. Can you help me?
Clerk Sure. What seems to be the problem?
Woman It's my camera. *I have no idea why it isn't working.*
Clerk Hmm. Let me look at it. It might be the battery. _____
Woman No, I can't. _____ I'm not sure if I've ever changed it.
Clerk Well, you definitely need a new one.
Woman _____
Clerk You need a 3.7 volt battery.
Woman _____
Clerk They're $39.99 each.
Woman Great. _____
Clerk Sure. They're at the back of the store. Here, let me show you.
Woman Thanks. _____ Maybe I should have an extra one.
Clerk That might be a good idea.

2 I wonder . . .

Grammar **A** **Tara wants to download some music from the Internet. Rewrite the questions she wants to ask her friend Kwang.**

1. I wonder *if you can download songs from this website* _____.
2. Can you tell me _____?
3. Do you know _____?
4. Do you have any idea _____?
5. Do you know _____?
6. Can you remember _____?
7. I wonder _____.
8. Do you know _____?

B **Kwang doesn't know the answers to Tara's questions. Write his replies using the expressions in the box. Use each expression twice.**

I don't know	I can't remember	I have no idea	I'm not sure

1. *I don't know if you can download songs from this website.*
2. _____
3. _____
4. _____
5. _____
6. _____
7. _____
8. _____

1 You should put it down.

Grammar and vocabulary **Complete the sentences with the phrasal verbs in the box. Add the correct pronouns.**

look up	put away	put on	take apart	throw away
print out	✓put down	set up	take off	turn off

1. Thanks for bringing in the box of groceries. Could you *put it down* over here?
2. I did something awful to my computer. I tried to _____, and now I can't get all the pieces back in it.
3. I hate those sticky price labels on things you buy. I can never _____.
4. My game controller doesn't work anymore. I wonder if I should just _____.
5. There's nothing good on TV. Do you mind if I _____?
6. I just bought these new headphones. Do you want to _____ and try them out?
7. I downloaded a video-chat app, but I can't _____.
8. I don't know what this word means. Maybe I should _____ on the Internet.
9. My brother leaves his video games all over the floor. He should _____, or they'll get damaged.
10. After you write documents, do you _____ to read them?

2 Step-by-step

Grammar and vocabulary **Complete the conversation with the words in the box.**

hook up / the computer	✓turn down / the air conditioning
pick up / the monitor	turn on / the radio
plug in / all the cables	turn up / the volume

Ruth We found this great apartment, but it's so cold in here.

Kate Oh, I'll *turn down the air conditioning*.
There we go. So, what do you want to do first?

Ruth Let's put some music on.
Can you _____?

Kate Sure. Is that loud enough?

Ruth Not really. Can you _____? Thanks.

Kate I'd like to _____, so I can check my email.

Ruth OK, let's put the computer over by the window.
I'll _____.
You get the computer and the cables.

Kate OK. You know, I have no idea where to _____.

Ruth I'm sure we can figure it out. Do you know where the manual is?

3 What to do?

Grammar and vocabulary

Complete the conversations using the given words. Write A's suggestions in two different ways. Then use the correct pronoun in B's response.

1. A Before you go out, *put on your hat and gloves* .
   Before you go out, *put your hat and gloves on* .
   (put on / your hat and gloves)
   B If I get too warm, can I *take them off* ?
   (take off)

2. A _____ in a dictionary.
   _____ in a dictionary.
   (look up / the new words)
   B Can we _____ on the Internet?
   (look up)

3. A You have to _____ gently.
   You have to _____ gently.
   (put in / the DVD)
   B If it doesn't work, should I _____ ?
   (take out)

4. A The kitchen's so messy. We should _____ .
   The kitchen's so messy. We should _____ .
   (put away / the dishes)
   B Actually, why don't we _____ ?
   (throw away)

4 About you

Grammar

Complete the questions. Then fill in the survey with true answers.

	Yes	No
1. Can you explain to someone *how to set up voice mail on a phone* ? (how / set up voice mail on a phone)	☐	☐
2. Do you have any idea _____ on your computer? (where / plug in the headphones)	☐	☐
3. Could you tell someone _____ ? (how / use your TV remote)	☐	☐
4. Do you know _____ on the Internet? (how / look up information)	☐	☐
5. Do you have any idea _____ when your computer crashes? (what / do)	☐	☐
6. Do you know _____ on your computer? (how / change the password)	☐	☐

Lesson C On the other hand, . . .

1 Don't you think . . . ?

Conversation strategies

A Match Cameron's opinions with her friends' responses.

1. I think kids watch too much TV. __f__
2. I think video games are totally boring and stupid. ____
3. I don't think people should drive big cars. ____
4. It's a shame no one writes letters anymore. I used to love getting them. ____
5. Kids need to spend less time on the computer. ____
6. I don't like shopping on the Internet. You can't see what you're buying. ____

a. I know what you mean, but with email, you can get in touch with people more often and faster.
b. I'm not so sure. Don't you think they can learn a lot online, too? I mean, there are some good educational websites.
c. Maybe. People with large families need to have big cars, though.
d. I don't know. I find it saves me time because I don't have to go to the store and wait in line.
e. I know what you mean, but there are so many different kinds of games. You could probably find something you liked.
f. That's true. On the other hand, kids need to relax sometimes, and we all have our favorite shows.

B Write your own responses to Cameron's opinions in part A. Use the expressions in the box if you disagree with her.

I know what you mean, but . . .	I don't know.
I'm not (so) sure. Don't you think . . . ?	✓That's true. . . . , though.
Maybe.	On the other hand, . . .

1. *That's true. I think some TV shows are educational, though.*
2. _____
3. _____
4. _____
5. _____
6. _____

2 What's your opinion?

Conversation strategies

Write opinions about the topics. Then add an expression from the box to get someone to agree with you. Use each expression twice.

You know what I mean? You know? You know what I'm saying?

1. Texting is *really convenient. But it's really annoying when you're trying to have a conversation with someone who's texting at the same time. You know what I mean?*
2. Video calling is _____
3. Blogging is _____
4. Online video clips are _____
5. Tablets are _____
6. Social networking is _____

3 I don't know.

Conversation strategies

Respond to each statement with a different opinion. Try to convince the other person to agree with you.

1. Kids spend too much time on the Internet.

   I don't know. I think it's great they learn how to use computers when they're so young. You know?

2. Teens shouldn't go to school and work at the same time. It's too hard.

   _____

3. I think too many people are addicted to their computers and phones and everything.

   _____

4. You never know if things you see on the Internet are true.

   _____

Lesson D Identity theft

1 Spam-a-lot

Reading **A Read the article. Then check (✓) the best title.**

☐ How to Be a Successful Spammer
☐ Where to Send Spam
☐ How Companies Avoid Spam
☐ Don't Be a Victim – How You Can Avoid Spam

Are you fed up with junk email and spam that fills up your inbox every day? Spam isn't just annoying for home users of computers. It's becoming a serious problem for businesses, too. Getting rid of spam wastes employees' time. Spam takes up space on computers, and it can slow down – or even jam – normal email traffic.

Most people don't know how spammers get their email address, but in fact, it's very easy. Your email address may be on any number of Internet sites such as blogs, email newsletters, company directories, and many other lists on the Web. You can also become a spam victim if you've entered an online contest or responded to a survey using your email address.

Spammers also use software that generates email addresses automatically. This software makes up millions of email addresses by using common names and the addresses of well-known companies and Internet service providers. It then sends out messages to all the addresses it creates. Although some of them might not work and the messages "bounce back," many others will get through to real people. The spammers now have a valuable list of valid addresses, which they can sell to other spammers at high prices.

HOW TO PROTECT YOURSELF FROM SPAM

DO:

- Change your email address regularly. Create an address that is difficult to guess. For example, if your name is Kevin Smith and you love cycling, try an address like KSmith4biking@cup.org. Or if you live in Toronto, you could use KS_in_Toronto@cup.org.
- Have two email addresses – one for public use and a private one only for friends and family.
- Buy anti-spam software or use email filters. Many email programs have filters that automatically send spam to a junk-mail folder. Be sure to check the junk-mail folder periodically for any personal mail that goes there by mistake.
- Pay attention to typos and misspellings in email subject lines. These are warning signs of possible spam.

DON'T:

- Respond to spam – ever. When you respond, you confirm that your address is valid.
- Buy anything from a company that sent you spam. This supports their belief that spamming makes money.

B Find the underlined words in the article. Then circle the best meaning.

1. Spam can <u>jam</u> normal email traffic.	a. slow down	(b.) stop or block
2. You can become a <u>spam victim</u>.	a. someone who gets spam	b. someone who sends spam
3. The software <u>generates</u> addresses.	a. creates	b. gets rid of
4. Some messages "<u>bounce back</u>."	a. get to the people	b. go back to the spammers
5. They have a list of <u>valid</u> addresses.	a. real	b. false
6. Never <u>confirm</u> your address.	a. forget	b. say it's correct

2 Get rid of it!

Writing **A Read the list of ideas, and add an idea of your own. Then use the ideas to complete the article.**

Ways to prevent spam

- Get another email address. Use one email address for chat rooms and message boards.
- Tell friends and family how to prevent spam.
- Use spam-filtering software.
- Don't respond to spam.
- _____
  _____
  _____

How to get rid of spam

First of all, keep your personal email address private. If you want to participate in chat rooms or on *message boards*, get a second _____ from a free email provider. Second, don't _____ to spam, even when it provides a link to "unsubscribe" from the list. Spammers see that your address is valid and sell it to other spammers. Third, use the _____ on your computer. Fourth, _____.

Finally, tell _____ about these tips. If fewer people respond to spam, there will be less spam!

B Brainstorm ideas on one of these topics. Then plan and write a short article.

- How to avoid identity theft
- How to protect yourself from theft
- How to use the Internet safely
- How to get help with computer problems

Ideas

_____
_____
_____
_____
_____

Unit 9 Progress chart

	What can you do? Mark the boxes. ✓ = I can . . . ? = I need to review how to . . .	To review, go back to these pages in the Student's Book.
Grammar	☐ use questions within questions and statements. ☐ use *how to*, *where to*, and *what to* + verb. ☐ use separable phrasal verbs like *turn on* and *plug in*.	86 and 87 88 88
Vocabulary	☐ use at least 12 phrasal verbs.	88 and 89
Conversation strategies	☐ use expressions to give a different opinion. ☐ use expressions to get someone to agree with me.	90 91
Writing	☐ brainstorm and organize ideas to plan an article.	93

What's up?

UNIT 10

Lesson A Catching up

1 What have they been doing?

Grammar **A** **What have these people been doing? What have they done? Complete the sentences using the present perfect continuous and then the present perfect.**

1. Kazuo *'s been doing yard work* (do yard work). He *'s planted* (plant) some flowers.

2. Sienna and Lynn _____ (shop). They _____ (spend) over $500 each!

3. Lola _____ (run). She _____ just _____ (finish) a marathon.

4. Carmen _____ (cook) dinner. She _____ (grill) some fish.

5. Sal and Elena _____ (ski). They _____ (have) one lesson.

6. Tony _____ (do) laundry all morning. He _____ (wash) three loads.

B **Circle the correct word to complete each sentence.**

1. Kazuo's been doing yard work **since** / **for** a few hours.
2. Sienna and Lynn haven't shopped online **since** / **in** months.
3. Lola's been running **since** / **for** she was in college.
4. Carmen hasn't made unhealthy food **since** / **in** a long time.
5. Sal and Elena have been skiing **since** / **for** this morning.
6. Tony's been doing the laundry **for** / **in** over two hours.

2 Questions, questions . . .

Grammar **Read each situation. Then use the words to write questions and answers in the present perfect continuous or the present perfect.**

1. You have a friend who has been taking Spanish lessons. You ask:
   A (how long / study / Spanish) *How long have you been studying Spanish?*
   B (seven months) *I've been studying Spanish for seven months.*
   A (how many words / learn) _____
   B (about 250) _____

2. You meet a famous baseball player. You ask:
   A (how long / play / baseball) _____
   B (18 years) _____
   A (how many games / win this season) _____
   B (12 out of 15) _____

3 About you

Grammar **A Complete the questions. Use the present perfect continuous or the present perfect.**

1. What *have* you *been doing* (do) lately after class?
2. How many times _____ you _____ (go) to the movies this month?
3. Who _____ you _____ (hang out) with recently?
4. How many times _____ you _____ (eat out) at a restaurant this week?
5. _____ you _____ (study) a lot lately?
6. How many phone calls _____ you _____ (make) this week?
7. How many times _____ you _____ (oversleep) in the last month?
8. What _____ you _____ (think) about for the last hour?
9. How many books _____ you _____ (read) this year?
10. _____ you _____ (exercise) lately?

B Answer the questions in part A with true information.

1. *I've been taking guitar lessons.*
2. _____
3. _____
4. _____
5. _____
6. _____
7. _____
8. _____
9. _____
10. _____

1 Crossword puzzle

Vocabulary **Complete the crossword puzzle.**

Across

2. A movie with an exciting story and lots of suspense is a *thriller* .
3. A _____ movie is about soldiers.
5. In a romantic _____ , two people fall in love and funny things happen.
7. A movie about a real event is called a _____ story.
9. A movie that makes you cry is called a tear_____ .
10. An _____ movie has a fast-moving story and is often violent.

Down

1. A _____ -fiction movie often takes place in the future.
4. A movie with cartoon characters is an _____ movie.
6. A movie that has singing and dancing is a _____ .
8. _____ movies are often scary and have monsters in them.

2 Best of Bollywood

Vocabulary **Complete Daria's blog with the words in the box.**

✓comedies	endings	love story	set in	subtitled
costumes	hilarious	play	stunts	take place

Daria's Blog

Daria 12:31 p.m.

Some of my favorite movies are musicals from Bollywood, especially the romantic *comedies* . The movies are usually _____ _____ India, and the actors often _____ characters who fall in love. I really enjoy a good _____ _____ . They can sometimes be tearjerkers, but the nice thing about Bollywood movies is that they often have happy _____ , so you leave the movie theater feeling good. Some of them are also very funny – the last one I saw was just _____ . Some of them are historical and _____ _____ in the past. These are my favorites because the colors and the _____ are wonderful. The movies aren't usually in English, but they're _____ , so you can read while you're watching. Sometimes the movies even have fight scenes with lots of special effects and _____ . They're really great!

3 About you

Vocabulary **Write reviews of movies you've seen. Complete each sentence with the title of a movie. Then write more about each one by answering the questions.**

CHOOSE A MOVIE	What type of movie is it? What's it about? Who's in it? Did you like it? Why? Why not?
1. I really enjoyed _____ *Les Misérables* _____.	*It's a musical, and it's set in France in the 1800s. Hugh Jackman plays a man who escapes from prison. Russell Crowe is the police officer who chases him. I really enjoyed the movie. It has wonderful music, and the costumes are amazing.*
2. _____ _____ is playing right now.	
3. The best movie I've ever seen is _____ _____.	
4. I didn't like _____ _____.	

4 I still haven't see it.

Grammar and vocabulary **Complete the conversation with *already*, *still*, or *yet*.**

Ann There are so many movies that I ___*still*___ haven't seen. Do you want to go see one tonight?

Gus Yeah, OK. Let's see. How about Brad Pitt's new movie? I haven't seen that _____.

Ann Oh, I've _____ seen that one. It was good. How about the new horror movie that's out? Have you seen that _____ ?

Gus No, I don't like scary movies. I'm 25, and I _____ haven't seen a horror movie.

Ann Well, there's a new animated movie out. I haven't seen that one _____ , either.

Gus Oh, great. Let's go. I've been dying to see it!

Lesson C I was wondering . . .

1 Favors

Conversation strategies **Complete the conversations with the expressions in the box.**

I wanted to	I was wondering,
✓ I was wondering if I could	Would it be all right if I
I was wondering if you could	Would it be OK

1. **Victor** Hi, Raoul. What can I do for you?
   Raoul *I was wondering if I could* _____ talk to you for a moment. Is now OK?
   Victor No problem. Come on in.
   Raoul Thanks. _____ worked from home tomorrow?
   Victor Tomorrow?
   Raoul Yes. Someone is coming to fix my stove, and I need to be home to let him in. _____ with you?
   Victor Yeah, sure. I don't see why not.
   Raoul Thanks, Victor. I really appreciate it.

2. **Dad** Hi, Josie. What's up?
   Josie Hey, Dad. _____ ask you a favor.
   Dad Sure, what is it?
   Josie Well, _____ lend me some money – if that's OK.
   Dad Hmm. It depends. How much? And for what?
   Josie Well, I was thinking, your birthday is next week, right?
   Dad Yes, it is.
   Josie So, _____ could I borrow $50 to buy you your present?

2 Can I borrow the car?

Conversation strategies

Stephanie's friend Ally is coming for a visit. Stephanie needs to ask her roommate Jenny for some favors. Look at her list, and complete each of her requests.

Things I need to do:

1. *Ask Jenny if Ally can stay here.*
2. *Pick up Ally at airport – borrow Jenny's car.*
3. *See if Jenny wants to go sightseeing with us Saturday.*
4. *Organize a party Saturday night – check with Jenny.*
5. *Check Ally's return flight online – use Jenny's computer.*

1. I wanted to *ask you if Ally could stay here* _____.
2. I was wondering if I could _____.
3. I was wondering, _____?
4. Would it be all right _____?
5. Would it be OK with you if I _____?

3 All right. What time?

Conversation strategies

Choose the best sentence to continue each conversation. Then write *A* if the speaker is agreeing, *M* if the speaker is moving the conversation along, or *U* to show the speaker understands.

1. A I'm going grocery shopping later, and I was wondering if you could come and help me. [A]
   B ☑ All right. What time?
   ☐ That's OK.

2. A Do you have time to talk now? [ ]
   B Sure. Let me just put these papers away.
   ☐ Um, OK, I guess so.
   ☐ All right. What did you want to talk about?

3. A This pasta is delicious! Could you give me the recipe? [ ]
   B ☐ Sure. It's very easy.
   ☐ That would be OK.

4. A Can you help me with something? [ ]
   B ☐ OK. What do you need?
   ☐ That's all right.

5. A I'm leaving early today. [ ]
   B ☐ Right. I remember you have an appointment.
   ☐ OK. I think so, too.

1 Weekend favorites

Reading **A Read the reviews. What things are reviewed? Check (✓) the boxes.**

☐ a book ☐ a movie ☐ a phone app ☐ a video game ☐ a Web app

Weekend Blog

THINGS TO KEEP YOU BUSY ON WEEKENDS

1. MOVIE EFFECTIVE

With Movie Effective, you can add special effects to your videos. Simply record a video with your smartphone camera. Then add exciting effects — just like they do in the movies. The app comes with two effects — lightning and slow motion — but you can also buy others, like sound effects. Even though I don't usually shoot or share videos personally, I found this to be a lot of fun. So, be careful — it's addictive, and you may get totally hooked!

2. *ACCUSED*

I really enjoyed playing this game. It combines a science-fiction setting with great action. You are a character who is wrongly accused of a crime. You have to find out who the real criminal is and get justice. Your choices determine the storyline. The action is fast-moving and there are some sad moments, so if you're very sensitive, this may not be the video game for you. However, the amazing setting and the ability to create your own story make this a great game for most players.

3. RECORDYOURRUN

If you are serious about running, hiking, biking, or even skiing, and have been wondering how to keep track of your progress, this phone app is the answer. It records your pace, distance, and time, and you can save your results and compare different exercise sessions. You can set goals for each time you go out and share your progress with friends. There's also a feature that lets your friends and family follow your progress in a race on a map. This app is the perfect way to mix technology and exercise.

4. FRETENDS

FretEnds has a fabulous Web app that will teach you how to play the guitar. You can choose to play a real guitar or a virtual one. There are eight levels of play. If you start at the beginner level, you will learn to play "Brown Eyed Girl." You need to let the app access the microphone on your computer, so it can "hear" you play. Each song is broken down into small parts. After you've learned one part, you can move on. This app is great for everyone, whether you've never played or even if you've been playing for years.

B Read the article again. Write *T* (true) or *F* (false) for each sentence. Then correct the false sentences.

1. Movie Effective helps you record videos on your smartphone. __F__
2. The special effects on Movie Effective are all free. ____
3. *Accused* is a romantic comedy. ____
4. *Accused* is suitable for everyone. ____
5. RecordYourRun is for people who take exercise seriously. ____
6. With RecordYourRun, people can see if their friends are winning a race. ____
7. You need to buy a guitar before you can use the FretEnds app. ____
8. The FretEnds app is not for experienced players. ____

2 Music review

Writing **A** **Read the music review. Complete the sentences with *although*, *even though*, or *even if* to contrast ideas. Sometimes more than one answer is possible.**

_____ *Come Away With Me* was amazingly successful and really introduced Norah Jones to the world, *Little Broken Hearts* is a much better album. Most of her earlier work uses a lot of piano, but this album focuses more on the guitar, so the sound is different. _____ most of these songs are about heartbreak, the music is beautiful and sweet. _____ you don't like sad romantic songs, you will find something to enjoy in this new collection.

– *Music Scene* magazine

B **Write a review of a movie, an album, or a TV show. Use *although*, *even though*, and *even if* to contrast ideas.**

Unit 10 Progress chart

	What can you do? Mark the boxes. ✓ = I can . . . ? = I need to review how to . . .	To review, go back to these pages in the Student's Book.
Grammar	☐ use the present perfect and present perfect continuous.	98 and 99
	☐ use *since*, *for*, and *in* with the present perfect to show duration.	99
	☐ use *already*, *still*, and *yet* with the present perfect.	101
Vocabulary	☐ name at least 6 different kinds of movies.	100 and 101
	☐ talk about movies using at least 15 new words and expressions.	100 and 101
Conversation strategies	☐ ask for a favor politely.	102
	☐ use *All right*, *OK*, and *Sure* to agree to requests; *All right*, *OK*, and *So* to move a conversation to a new phase or topic; and *Right* to show I agree or understand.	103
Writing	☐ use *although*, *even though*, and *even if* to contrast ideas.	105

Impressions

UNIT 11

Lesson A Speculating

1 It could be . . .

Grammar **Complete the sentences with the expressions in the box. Then write a second sentence using the cues and an appropriate modal.**

can't be the winners	may be taking a driving test	✓ must be learning to drive
could be taking a hard test	might be the best student	must be the winners

1. He *must be learning to drive* _____.
   It could / might / may be his first lesson.
   (It / be / his first lesson)

2. He _____.
   _____
   (It / be / his first lesson)

3. She _____.
   _____
   (She / feel proud)

4. She _____.
   _____
   (She / be nervous)

5. They _____.
   _____
   (They / practice a lot)

6. They _____.
   _____
   (They / be disappointed)

2 He must be crazy!

Grammar **Circle the correct words to complete the sentences.**

1. Mandy What's he doing? He **must be** / **can't be** crazy!
   Molly He **might be** / **can't be** an acrobat with the circus.
   Mandy You're right. He **must practice** / **must be practicing** for tonight's show.
   Molly That's amazing! I mean, it **can't be** / **might be** easy to bend like that.
   Mandy Yeah, it **could be** / **must not be** painful, too.
   Molly Well, I certainly won't try that!

2. Jason How old is that kid? She **must be** / **can't be** more than five years old.
   Peter Yeah, you're right. She **must not be** / **might be** about four or five.
   Jason She's really good. She **must play** / **must be playing** every day for hours and hours.
   Peter She makes it look so easy, too. I wonder what her parents think. They **could be** / **must be** so proud.
   Jason Yeah, she **could be** / **can't be** the youngest professional piano player in the world.

3 About you

Grammar **Think of someone you know who is not in the room with you now. Answer the questions about him or her using *must*, *may*, *might*, *could*, or *can't*.**

1. Where do you think he or she is right now?
   It's Saturday afternoon, so he might be on the golf course. He can't be at work.
2. What do you think he or she is doing?
   _____
3. How do you think he or she is feeling?
   _____
4. What do you think he or she is wearing?
   _____
5. Who do you think he or she is with?
   _____
6. What do you think he or she is thinking about right now?
   _____

Lesson B Ups and downs

1 Scrambled up

Grammar and vocabulary

A **Write the adjective for each definition. You can check your answers in a dictionary. Then use the letters in the boxes to answer the question below.**

1. Greatly surprised _a_ _m_ [a] _z_ _e_ _d_
2. Upset or not pleased ___ ___ [ ] ___ ___ ___ ___
3. Makes you feel excited ___ [ ] ___ ___ ___ ___ ___ ___
4. Irritating ___ ___ ___ ___ ___ ___ ___ ___ [ ] ___ ___
5. Not interesting ___ [ ] ___ ___ ___ ___
6. Not expected or normal ___ [ ] ___ ___ ___ ___ ___ ___ ___ ___
7. Frightening [ ] ___ ___ ___ ___

How might you feel the first time you try something new? _a_ ___ ___ ___ ___ ___ ___

B **Complete the sentences with the other forms of the adjectives in part A.**

1. Someone who upsets you or makes you slightly angry is _annoying_ .
2. If someone gives you a present for no reason, you might be _____ .
3. If you have nothing to do, you might feel _____ .
4. When you're very afraid of something, you might feel _____ .
5. Someone who learns to speak six or seven languages is truly _____ .
6. When you're going to do something fun, you are _____ about it.
7. When you can't remember a word in English, you probably feel _____ .

2 Good news, bad news

Grammar and vocabulary **Complete the emails. Use the correct forms of the adjectives.**

New Message

To: EmmaP@cup.com
From: shak91@cup.com
Subject: My short story

Hey Emma,

I'm so *excited* (excite). Remember the short story I wrote for English class last month? Well, my teacher sent it to a competition, and guess what? It won first prize! The judges said my story was very _____ (interest). I knew my teacher was _____ (please) with my work. She said my story was _____ (fascinate). But I never thought she would enter it in a competition! I was totally _____ (shock) when she told me. And all my classmates were totally _____ (jealous). What's new and exciting with you?

Shakira

New Message

To: shak91@cup.com
From: EmmaP@cup.com
Subject: My short story

Hi Shakira,

Congratulations! I wish I had _____ (excite) news for you, too, but I don't. Unfortunately, I failed my driver's test last week. I was really _____ (disappoint). It's just so _____ (embarrass) – it's the third time I've failed the test. The driving instructor told me to make a right-hand turn, and I turned left instead. I guess I got a little _____ (confuse). I could tell the instructor was really _____ (annoy) with me! My dad told me not to get _____ (frustrate). He said he failed his driver's test five times before he finally passed, but I'm starting to get _____ (worry). Well, talk to you later.

Emma

3 About you

Grammar and vocabulary **How would you feel in these situations? Complete the sentences with true information.**

1. You fail a test that you have studied very hard for.
   I would feel *disappointed if I failed a test that I thought I was prepared for* _____.
   It might be *embarrassing if my friends found out* _____.
2. Your friend doesn't show up for a date.
   I would get _____.
   I might feel _____.
3. You are home alone during a storm.
   I might feel _____.
   It could be _____.
4. Someone is telling you a story you've already heard ten times.
   I might feel _____.
   I would probably think _____.

Lesson C That must be fun.

1 You must be excited.

Conversation strategies **Complete the responses in the conversations to show understanding. Use *must be* and an adjective.**

1. I'm learning how to design a website. *That must be hard* _____.
2. My brother always takes my stuff. That _____.
3. I lost my wallet and credit cards at the mall. You _____.
4. I'm going to climb Mount Rainier next month. You _____.
5. I didn't win the poetry contest. You _____.
6. My ex-boyfriend is dating my best friend. That _____.

2 Explanations

Conversation strategies **Complete the conversation with *you see* or *I see*, or leave a blank where neither one is appropriate.**

Walt Hi, Reg. I'm sorry I'm late. I didn't hear my alarm. *You see* _____, I was working on my report until about 3:30 this morning.

Reg Uh-huh, _____. So, will it be ready for the meeting with the boss?

Walt _____ Yes. I just have to make some copies. What time is the meeting?

Reg Well, it was at 11:00, but the boss called me about half an hour ago, and it's now at 2:30. She's meeting someone for lunch, _____, and she has to leave at 11:30.

Walt Oh, _____. So, I guess I didn't have to rush.

Reg Well, at least it's all done now, and you can relax.

3 An author in Paris

Conversation strategies **Complete the conversation with the expressions in the box. Use each expression twice.**

I see | that must be | you must be | you see

Akina Hey, Omar. I hear you're going away for a while. Where to?

Omar Yeah, I'm leaving for Paris next week.

Akina You're kidding! Wow, *you must be* excited!

Omar I am. I've never been there before. _____, I'm going to do some research for my next book. That's always the best part – the research.

Akina I bet. _____ fun. So, what's your book about?

Omar It's a love story, of course.

Akina _____. Uh . . . can you share any details yet?

Omar I guess. Hmm . . . let's see. It's about a young girl who goes to visit a friend in Paris. And well, you know, she meets a mysterious young man, they fall in love, and lots of things happen.

Akina Really? What kind of things?

Omar Well, I don't want to say yet. _____, I want to keep the details a surprise.

Akina I understand. But, gosh, _____ hard. I can never keep secrets.

Omar I know what you mean. It's difficult sometimes.

Akina So, tell me what else you're doing in Paris.

Omar Oh. I'm going to read from my last novel at an English-language bookstore.

Akina Great! _____ pleased about that. Will you be nervous?

Omar No, not at all. I've done it several times. It's part of the job of being a writer.

Akina _____. Well, have a wonderful trip. Good luck with your research.

Omar Thanks. I'll tell you all about it when I get back.

1 Child prodigies

Reading **A Read the article. What does "child prodigy" mean?**

☐ someone under the age of 15 ☐ a child with a special talent ☐ a child who is famous

CHILD PRODIGIES:

Nature OR Nurture?

Mozart wrote his first minuet at age six. Cellist Yo-Yo Ma first performed in public at the age of five. William James Sidis read Homer in Greek at age four and was the youngest person ever to attend Harvard University at 11. Ukrainian chess player Sergey Karjakin became the youngest international grand master at 12. Pablo Picasso first publicly exhibited his paintings at age 13.

Many parents may hope for a genius child, but there can be a price to pay. Some child prodigies never experience a normal childhood, often because it's difficult for them to make friends, and they suffer socially. Some genius children even have mental breakdowns at an early age, and gifted child athletes or musicians can be permanently injured from practicing too hard.

We often hear stories of parents who push their children too hard. However, some experts say that for the most part, "pushy parent" is an unfair label: Parents don't push prodigies, prodigies push parents. Many gifted children quickly become bored with school and homework that is too easy. For these kids, school is frustrating, and they risk losing interest in it altogether. It's better to allow these children to skip grades, experts say, than to let them become disappointed in school.

Are prodigies born, or are they created? The short answer is: we don't know. Certainly, many parents of gifted children provide a stimulating environment: They read to their children at an early age, take them to museums and concerts, and give them a lot of independence. But experts advise parents not to be disappointed if their child isn't an early genius. Mozart was a child prodigy; Einstein was not. But the world is still amazed by them both.

B Find a word or expression in the article for each meaning below.

1. go to, or be present at (a place or an event) (paragraph 1) *attend*
2. psychological problems (paragraph 2) _____
3. talented; exceptional (paragraph 3) _____
4. interesting; encouraging you to learn (paragraph 4) _____

C Read the article again. Then answer the questions.

1. Who's the youngest prodigy mentioned in the article?

   _____

2. What are three disadvantages of being a child prodigy?

   _____

3. What problems do some gifted children have with school?

   _____

4. How do some parents help their gifted children develop?

   _____

2 My child is a prodigy!

Writing **A Read the letter from a parent to a school principal. Circle the expressions that give impressions or opinions. Underline the statements that are stated as fact.**

MT

Dear Dr. Evans,

My child is enrolled in your school. I believe that he is a very gifted student, and I feel that he is bored in his classes. It seems to me that he is becoming increasingly frustrated and anxious because he has lost interest in school. Last year he was the top student in his class, but this year his grades are slipping. My impression is that he needs to take more difficult classes. In my opinion, he is not finding his current classes challenging enough. Can you help?

Sincerely,

Marsha Taylor

B Write a letter to the editor of a local newspaper about one of the topics below or your own idea. Use the expressions from part A.

- There aren't enough leisure facilities for local teens.
- We need healthier food options in schools.
- There's too much litter on city streets.

Unit 11 Progress chart

	What can you do? Mark the boxes. ✓ = I can . . . ? = I need to review how to . . .	To review, go back to these pages in the Student's Book.
Grammar	☐ use the modals *must, may, might, can't,* and *could* to speculate.	108 and 109
	☐ use adjectives ending in *-ed* to describe how someone feels.	110 and 111
	☐ use adjectives ending in *-ing* to describe someone or something.	110 and 111
Vocabulary	☐ name at least 12 adjectives to describe feelings and reactions.	110 and 111
Conversation strategies	☐ use *That must be* or *You must be* + adjective to show I understand.	112
	☐ use *You see* to explain something and *I see* to show I understand.	113
Writing	☐ use expressions like *I feel* to give impressions or opinions.	115

In the news

UNIT 12

Lesson A Local news

1 And now, the news . . .

Grammar **Complete the news reports. Use the simple past passive.**

1. Newtown Park train station *was closed* (close) this morning after a bag _____ (find) on a train. Several trains _____ (delay), and some _____ (cancel). The bag _____ (remove) from the station and _____ (search). Police said later that the bag was full of clothes. The train station _____ (reopen) after two hours.

2. A woman _____ (rescue) earlier today after she climbed onto her roof to repair her chimney. Firefighters _____ (call) to the scene after neighbors heard the woman shout for help. Fortunately, the woman _____ (not hurt), but she _____ (take) to the local hospital and _____ (release) later this afternoon.

3. The National Museum _____ (break into) last night, and three valuable paintings _____ (steal). The area around the museum _____ (close off) following the incident, and bystanders _____ (interview). Police are now looking for two young men who _____ (see) nearby.

2 More news

Grammar **Rewrite the sentences using the simple past passive.**

1. They delayed the game for two hours. *The game was delayed for two hours.*
2. Someone stole a ring from an exhibit. _____
3. They canceled the rock concert. _____
4. A woman found a wallet on a bus. _____
5. They took two people to the hospital. _____
6. Someone rescued a man from a fire. _____

3 What happened?

Grammar **Look at the picture. What do you think happened? Write a news report. Use the verbs in the box or your own ideas. Use the simple past passive. Be creative with your facts!**

break into
close
find
hurt
open
rob
steal
take

News Report: Stolen Goods!

A downtown jewelry store was robbed yesterday.

Lesson B Natural disasters

1 All kinds of weather

Vocabulary **Look at the pictures. Complete the sentences with the words in the box.**

aftershocks	floods	hurricane	✓rains	tornado
earthquake	hailstorm	lightning	thunderstorm	winds

1. The region was hit by heavy ___*rains*___ earlier today. Several roads were closed because of flash _____ .

2. Farmers say their crops were badly damaged by the ice from a freak _____ that passed through the area today.

3. Parts of the country were damaged by a _____ yesterday.

4. Airports were closed today due to _____ Albert. Flights were canceled because of strong _____ and rain.

5. The area was hit yesterday by a major _____ , measuring 5.6 on the Richter scale. _____ were felt throughout the area.

6. Electricity throughout the city was disrupted by thunder and _____ from a severe _____ .

2 What was the cause?

Grammar and vocabulary

Look at each pair of pictures. What caused the damage? Write a sentence using the given word and *by*.

1. *A fire was started by a candle.*

2. _____

3. _____

4. _____

5. _____

3 In the news

Grammar

Rewrite the sentences using the simple past passive and the adverb given.

1. The fire damaged the building. (partially)
   The building was partially damaged by the fire.
2. The storm disrupted train services. (temporarily)
   _____
3. Flash floods damaged several houses in the area. (badly)
   _____
4. A wildfire injured three firefighters. (seriously)
   _____
5. A tornado destroyed a small farm. (completely)
   _____

Lesson C Did you hear about . . . ?

1 News travels fast!

Conversation strategies **Complete the conversation with the expressions in the box. Use each expression only once.**

did I tell you	guess what	you know
did you hear about	✓ have you heard	you know what

Don *Have you heard* _____ the news about Henry?

Nadia No. What happened to him?

Don Well, _____ he goes mountain biking, right?

Nadia Yes. I've seen him on his bike a lot.

Don Well, he went out biking yesterday, and _____? He was in the mountains during that big thunderstorm in the afternoon. He had to sit under a tree to avoid the lightning. . . .

Nadia Under a tree? _____? That's really dangerous.

Don It is?

Nadia Oh, yeah. _____ those golfers who were hit by lightning under a tree?

Don No. Oh, that's awful.

Nadia Yeah. They were taken to the hospital and everything. But amazingly, they were OK.

Don That was lucky. By the way, _____ about my car? The roof was damaged in that storm, too. It was hit by the hailstones.

2 About you

Conversation strategies **Write sentences introducing some news. Use true information.**

1. *You know my friend Callie? She got a new laptop for her birthday.*
(good news about a friend)

2. _____
(fun news about yourself)

3. _____
(bad news about a local sports team)

4. _____
(news about the local weather)

5. _____
(interesting news about your favorite actor or singer)

6. _____
(news about a family member)

7. _____
(news about another city)

3 The funny thing was . . .

Conversation strategies **Circle the best way to complete each sentence.**

1. I lost my bag last week, and then I found it outside my dorm room. The funny thing was, **everything was stolen** / **nothing was stolen**.
2. Thieves broke into my car last week, and the worst thing was, **they took my favorite bag** / **the inside of the car was completely cleaned**.
3. Some neighbors of ours got married last month, and the weird thing is, **they didn't tell anyone about it** / **we all had a great time**.
4. We had a great weekend at the beach. The best thing was, **the water was so warm** / **it rained**.
5. That movie was incredible. The only thing was, **the ending was the best** / **the ending was disappointing**.
6. We went out for dinner last night, and the food was terrible. The other thing was, **the waiters were helpful** / **it was really expensive**.

4 The whole story

Conversation strategies **Complete the conversations with the expressions in the box.**

Did I tell you?	The best thing is,
✓Did you hear	The funny thing is,

1. A *Did you hear* _____ about the new vacation schedule?
   B No, I didn't. What about it?
   A We get an extra week of vacation.
   B Great!
   A _____ the extra week is in February. That means we can plan a nice, long ski vacation!

2. A _____ There was a small fire at school yesterday.
   B Really? Where?
   A It was in the science lab. Some students were doing an experiment, and it exploded.
   B I hope no one was hurt.
   A Everyone is fine. _____ the students all got A's!

1 Only the news that interests you

Reading **A** **Read the article. Which news sources do young people use?**

CHANGING SOURCES OF NEWS

Far fewer people, especially the young, get their news from traditional news sources (either print or television), according to the most recent surveys. Instead, they are getting news from online sources and social networking sites, using their cell phones, tablets, and other mobile devices. In just two years, the number of people who get news from social networks doubled, and now about a third of young readers get their news this way. Although half of all Americans still watch TV to keep up with events, only 28% of people between the ages of 18 and 29 do so.

This use of social networks for news can be seen in Europe also. One in five people in the United Kingdom, and 43% of young people, get their news from the most popular social networking and microblogging sites. According to a recent study in Spain, three-quarters of the people between the ages of 16 and 30 got their news from a social networking site, as compared to only 28% from newspapers.

The addition of these news channels may contribute to "news fatigue," or a feeling of being overloaded with news. A study that was conducted by the University of Texas found that the way we get the news affects whether we feel information overload. People who got their news from computers and tablets were much more likely to feel overloaded, while people who got their news from TV or read it on their cell phone were less likely to experience this. The study showed that reading the same news on a computer was felt to be more tiring than reading it on a phone, perhaps because options seem more limited on a phone, and so more manageable. People on computers and tablets usually see many more links than people who use phone apps.

News organizations have adapted their news presentation style to try to prevent or reduce news fatigue. Some provide news in three forms: breaking headlines, short present-tense stories, and links to longer stories. By cutting down the number of headline updates, they also hope to reduce news fatigue.

B **Read the article again. Circle the best alternatives to complete the sentences.**

1. The author suggests in the article that young people and older people ____ .
   a. get news the same way (b.) often get their news from different sources
2. One news source that is growing in popularity is ____ .
   a. microblogging sites b. television news
3. Three out of four young people get their news from social networks in ____ .
   a. Spain b. the United States
4. People who get their news on computers are more likely to be overloaded than if they get their news on ____ .
   a. tablets b. smartphones
5. One way that people get news fatigue is by reading too many ____ .
   a. headline updates b. longer stories

2 News survey

Writing **A Read the survey. Then complete the article below with the expressions in the box.**

Barnesville News Survey:

1. Do you read the *Barnesville News* every day? **Yes** 49% **No** 51%
2. What's your favorite section?

Weather	0%
Local	9%
Sports	10%
Arts	20%
International	59%
Travel	2%

almost
✓ half
majority
none
out of
20%

About ___half___ of the people we surveyed read the *Barnesville News* every day. The _____ of *Barnesville News* readers prefer the international section. Only one _____ ten readers chose the sports section as their favorite. _____ 10% of readers enjoy the local section, while _____ of them are interested in the arts section. _____ of them chose the weather as their favorite.

B How many of your friends read a local or national news website? Write a paragraph like the one in part A to show the statistics.

Unit 12 Progress chart

What can you do? Mark the boxes. ☑ = I can . . . ? = I need to review how to . . .	To review, go back to these pages in the Student's Book.
Grammar	
☐ use the simple past passive to discuss the news.	118, 119, and 120
☐ use the passive + *by* to introduce the "doer" or cause of an action.	120 and 121
Vocabulary	
☐ name at least 10 types of extreme weather or natural disasters.	120 and 121
☐ name at least 4 adverbs with the simple past passive.	120 and 121
Conversation strategies	
☐ introduce news with expressions like *Guess what?*	122
☐ use expressions like *The thing is . . .* to introduce issues.	123
Writing	
☐ write about statistics.	125

Illustration credits

Harry Briggs: 22, 42, 80 **Cambridge University Press:** 21, 50 **Steve Cancel:** 93 **Chuck Gonzales:** 13, 37, 58, 82, 83 **Frank Montagna:** 2, 26, 27, 44, 67, 86, 87 **Marilena Perilli:** 6, 7, 20, 28, 46, 62, 63, 74 **Greg White:** 14, 35, 78, 91 **Terry Wong:** 5, 38, 39, 54, 68, 69, 94, 95

Photo credits

3 ©Andresr/Shutterstock **4** ©Erin Patrice O'Brien/Getty **8** *(top to bottom)* ©Michael Tran/FilmMagic/Getty Images; ©Eros International/courtesy Everett Collection **9** ©Monirul Alam/ZUMAPRESS.com/Alamy **10** *(left to right)* ©Alexandra Lande/Shutterstock; ©GoodSportHD.com/Alamy **11** ©Eyecandy Images/Alamy **12** *(top to bottom)* ©Yadid Levy/age fotostock/SuperStock; ©Andrew Bain/Getty Images; ©Manfred Grebler/Getty Images; ©Universal Images Group/SuperStock **15** *(left to right)* ©Philip Lee Harvey/Getty Images; ©Punchstock **16** *(top to bottom)* ©Oktay Ortakcioglu/Getty Images; ©leungchopan/Shutterstock **18** *(top row, left to right)* ©Francesco Dazzi/Shutterstock; ©Medioimages/Photodisc/Thinkstock; ©Maurilio Cheli/Associated Press; ©Max Nash/Associated Press *(bottom row, left to right)* ©Jerritt Clark/WireImage/Getty Images; ©Randy Faris/Corbis; ©Alik Keplicz/Associated Press; ©Mike Segar/Reuters/Newscom **19** ©Andrzej Gorzkowski Photography/Alamy **20** *(clockwise from top left)* ©Punchstock; ©Thinkstock; ©Digital Vision/Thinkstock; ©Thinkstock; ©AAMIR QURESHI/AFP/Getty Images; ©Galen Rowell/Corbis **23** ©Thinkstock **24** ©Photo Courtesy of NOAA *(background)* ©Serg Zastavkin/Shutterstock *(icicles)* ©April Cat/Shutterstock **25** ©Thinkstock **29** ©imagebroker.net/SuperStock **32** ©Frank Herholdt/Getty Images **34** ©George Kerrigan **35** ©George Kerrigan **36** *(top to bottom)* ©ifong/Shutterstock; ©Stockvision/Shutterstock **40** ©Thinkstock **41** *(top to bottom)* ©Robyn Mackenzie/Shutterstock; ©Lucky Business/Shutterstock **50** *(top to bottom)* ©Thinkstock; ©Punchstock; ©Dennis MacDonald/Age Fotostock; ©Sherrianne Talon/istockphoto; ©Jurgen Reisch/Getty Images **53** ©Rich Legg/Getty Images **55** *(all photos)* ©Thinkstock **59** ©x7vector/Shutterstock **61** ©Andrew D. Bernstein/NBAE via Getty Images **62** ©John Giustina/Getty Images **66** ©MediaBakery **70** ©PBS/Courtesy: Everett Collection **75** ©Clark Brennan/Alamy **77** ©Jupiterimages/Thinkstock **80** *(top)* ©DircinhaSW/Getty Images *(bottom, left to right)* ©JGI/Getty Images/RF; ©Cultura Limited/SuperStock **81** ©David Wolff-Patrick/WireImage/Getty Images **84** *(clockwise from top left)* ©Punchstock; ©Nick Chaldakov/Alamy; ©Thinkstock; ©Digital Vision/Thinkstock **90** *(top to bottom)* ©Mike Finn-Kelcey/Newscom; ©RubberBall/SuperStock; ©Thinkstock **92** *(clockwise from top left)* ©Sandra Mu/Getty Images; ©David Cole/Alamy; ©Thinkstock; ©Thinkstock; ©Thinkstock; ©Eric Nguyen/Jim Reed Photography/Corbis

Text credits

While every effort has been made, it has not always been possible to identify the sources of all the materials used, or to trace all copyright holders. If any omissions are brought to our notice, we will be happy to include the appropriate acknowledgements on reprinting.

The top 500 spoken words

This is a list of the top 500 words in spoken North American English. It is based on a sample of four and a half million words of conversation from the Cambridge International Corpus. The most frequent word, *I*, is at the top of the list.

1. I
2. and
3. the
4. you
5. uh
6. to
7. a
8. that
9. it
10. of
11. yeah
12. know
13. in
14. like
15. they
16. have
17. so
18. was
19. but
20. is
21. it's
22. we
23. huh
24. just
25. oh
26. do
27. don't
28. that's
29. well
30. for
31. what
32. on
33. think
34. right
35. not
36. um
37. or
38. my
39. be
40. really
41. with
42. he
43. one
44. are
45. this
46. there
47. I'm
48. all
49. if
50. no
51. get
52. about
53. at
54. out
55. had
56. then
57. because
58. go
59. up
60. she
61. when
62. them
63. can
64. would
65. as
66. me
67. mean
68. some
69. good
70. got
71. OK
72. people
73. now
74. going
75. were
76. lot
77. your
78. time
79. see
80. how
81. they're
82. kind
83. here
84. from
85. did
86. something
87. too
88. more
89. very
90. want
91. little
92. been
93. things
94. an
95. you're
96. said
97. there's
98. I've
99. much
100. where
101. two
102. thing
103. her
104. didn't
105. other
106. say
107. back
108. could
109. their
110. our
111. guess
112. yes
113. way
114. has
115. down
116. we're
117. any

118. he's
119. work
120. take
121. even
122. those
123. over
124. probably
125. him
126. who
127. put
128. years
129. sure
130. can't
131. pretty
132. gonna
133. stuff
134. come
135. these
136. by
137. into
138. went
139. make
140. than
141. year
142. three
143. which
144. home
145. will
146. nice
147. never
148. only
149. his
150. doing
151. cause
152. off
153. I'll
154. maybe
155. real
156. why
157. big
158. actually
159. she's
160. day
161. five
162. always
163. school
164. look
165. still
166. around
167. anything
168. kids
169. first
170. does
171. need
172. us
173. should
174. talking
175. last
176. thought
177. doesn't
178. different
179. money
180. long
181. used
182. getting
183. same
184. four
185. every
186. new
187. everything
188. many
189. before
190. though
191. most
192. tell
193. being
194. bit
195. house
196. also
197. use
198. through
199. feel
200. course
201. what's
202. old
203. done
204. sort
205. great
206. bad
207. we've
208. another
209. car
210. true
211. whole
212. whatever
213. twenty
214. after
215. ever
216. find
217. care
218. better
219. hard
220. haven't
221. trying
222. give
223. I'd
224. problem
225. else
226. remember
227. might
228. again
229. pay
230. try
231. place
232. part
233. let
234. keep
235. children
236. anyway
237. came
238. six
239. family
240. wasn't
241. talk
242. made
243. hundred
244. night
245. call
246. saying

247. dollars
248. live
249. away
250. either
251. read
252. having
253. far
254. watch
255. week
256. mhm
257. quite
258. enough
259. next
260. couple
261. own
262. wouldn't
263. ten
264. interesting
265. am
266. sometimes
267. bye
268. seems
269. heard
270. goes
271. called
272. point
273. ago
274. while
275. fact
276. once
277. seen
278. wanted
279. isn't
280. start
281. high
282. somebody
283. let's
284. times
285. guy
286. area
287. fun
288. they've
289. you've
290. started
291. job
292. says
293. play
294. usually
295. wow
296. exactly
297. took
298. few
299. child
300. thirty
301. buy
302. person
303. working
304. half
305. looking
306. someone
307. coming
308. eight
309. love
310. everybody
311. able
312. we'll
313. life
314. may
315. both
316. type
317. end
318. least
319. told
320. saw
321. college
322. ones
323. almost
324. since
325. days
326. couldn't
327. gets
328. guys
329. god
330. country
331. wait
332. yet
333. believe
334. thinking
335. funny
336. state
337. until
338. husband
339. idea
340. name
341. seven
342. together
343. each
344. hear
345. help
346. nothing
347. parents
348. room
349. today
350. makes
351. stay
352. mom
353. sounds
354. change
355. understand
356. such
357. gone
358. system
359. comes
360. thank
361. show
362. thousand
363. left
364. friends
365. class
366. already
367. eat
368. small
369. boy
370. paper
371. world
372. best
373. water
374. myself
375. run

376. they'll
377. won't
378. movie
379. cool
380. news
381. number
382. man
383. basically
384. nine
385. enjoy
386. bought
387. whether
388. especially
389. taking
390. sit
391. book
392. fifty
393. months
394. women
395. month
396. found
397. side
398. food
399. looks
400. summer
401. hmm
402. fine
403. hey
404. student
405. agree
406. mother
407. problems
408. city
409. second
410. definitely
411. spend
412. happened
413. hours
414. war
415. matter
416. supposed
417. worked
418. company
419. friend
420. set
421. minutes
422. morning
423. between
424. music
425. close
426. leave
427. wife
428. knew
429. pick
430. important
431. ask
432. hour
433. deal
434. mine
435. reason
436. credit
437. dog
438. group
439. turn
440. making
441. American
442. weeks
443. certain
444. less
445. must
446. dad
447. during
448. lived
449. forty
450. air
451. government
452. eighty
453. wonderful
454. seem
455. wrong
456. young
457. places
458. girl
459. happen
460. sorry
461. living
462. drive
463. outside
464. bring
465. easy
466. stop
467. percent
468. hand
469. gosh
470. top
471. cut
472. computer
473. tried
474. gotten
475. mind
476. business
477. anybody
478. takes
479. aren't
480. question
481. rather
482. twelve
483. phone
484. program
485. without
486. moved
487. gave
488. yep
489. case
490. looked
491. certainly
492. talked
493. beautiful
494. card
495. walk
496. married
497. anymore
498. you'll
499. middle
500. tax